THROUGH THE HOOP

A Season with the Celtics

Pamela R. Schuyler

Interviews with Tom "Satch" Sanders

1974

HOUGHTON MIFFLIN COMPANY BOSTON

Library of Congress Cataloging in Publication Data

Schuyler, Pamela R
   Through the hoop.

   SUMMARY: Follows the Boston Celtics through an entire
season, at home and on the road, from training camp to
the playoffs, with glimpses of their thoughts and emotions.
   1. Boston Celtics (Basketball team)—Juvenile litera-
ture. [1. Boston Celtics (Basketball team) 2. Basket-
ball]. I. Sanders, Tom. II. Title.
GV885.52.B67S38   796.32'364'0974461   74-9380
ISBN 0-395-19920-4

Contents

1820785

To My Parents, Who Have Encouraged Me

With special thanks to:

John Nelson
and
David Cowens
Howie McHugh
Jeff Cohen
Jan Volk
Frank Challant
Red Auerbach
John Killilea
Tom Heinsohn
Don Chaney
Hank Finkel
Don Nelson
Jo Jo White
Artie Williams
Paul Westphal
John Havlicek

Paul Silas
Steve Kuberski
Phil Hankinson
Steve Downing
Walter Randall
Bob Ryan
Larry Whiteside
Ellis Herwig
George Kimball
Lenny Megliolia
Chris Gallagher
Don Mitchell
Andi and John Moselle

and all my other friends
who have helped me with
this book.

Introduction

Many people think playing basketball is just a matter of running, jumping, and shooting. They are not far from the truth. To be correct, however, you must modify that formula to read: *specified* running, *timely* jumping, and *selective* shooting. These terms tell you what the game is really about.

This book will add to your knowledge of professional basketball; it will touch on the thoughts and feelings of men who earn their bread and butter by playing this game.

A professional ballplayer's season begins when the last game of the current campaign has ended; immediately he starts to think about the next season. The veteran worries about his contract and about whether he can maintain or improve upon his previous season's performance. A rookie (or his agent) will· be negotiating his contract; once that's done, he faces the challenge of making the team.

The mental preparation has begun. It will be followed, for a rookie, by a lot of physical work and, for a veteran, by some rest and recuperation and a return to the basketball court sometime in August to get ready for training camp.

Whether you are a veteran or a rookie in the game of basketball, come along and take a full-court trip, in photographs and words, with the Boston Celtics.

THOMAS E. "SATCH" SANDERS

Training Camp

Played almost everywhere in the world today, basketball is the only major sport with undisputed origin in the United States. Professional basketball, as played by the teams in the National Basketball Association (NBA), begins each year in early fall at training camp.

NBA training camp lasts approximately one month, usually beginning around the middle of September. The first two weeks are spent at the campsite, the last two on the road for exhibition games.

Ballplayers live a spartan dormitory existence for the first two weeks. During this time, certain rules are observed, including:

No hard drinking. Alcohol can seriously impair an athlete's efficiency by placing added stress on his body system.

No female company. Many coaches feel that women distract a player's concentration.

No overeating. Diet is carefully controlled to keep the athlete healthy and active.

Smoking is frowned upon. Athletes who smoke cut down or stop. Smoking can damage the lungs and heart, which provide hungry muscles with the oxygen necessary to sustain them in peak condition during training camp's rigorous regimen.

Training camp is primarily a testing ground; a player has to prepare himself mentally as well as physically for this situation. A rookie can encounter difficulties in adjusting to the differences between college and professional ball. Accustomed to a season of thirty games, he now faces an eighty-two game schedule. He must get ready for more physical contact from larger men, shooting within twenty-four seconds, playing with a wider three-second lane, as well as the fact that he is up against consistently exceptional opponents (not just one standout per team, as may have been true in college). To gain a head start on this adjustment, many players seek out pro-style summer tournaments, such as the Rucker Tourney in New York City, the Los Angeles Summer League in California, or the Baker Tournament in Philadelphia.

When a man decides to become a professional ballplayer he must have the desire to play no matter what. The *what* can mean anything from performing for less money than he thinks he deserves to playing when severely handicapped by injuries. He walks into training camp knowing that almost all the veterans are returning. He must believe he can displace one of them.

The coach opens the initial session by stating: "The door is wide open." Every position is available (this will not be the whole truth if the team has one or more veterans of outstanding ability or if some rookies have successfully negotiated long-term, no-cut contracts). Anyone can make the team if he is good enough, however, and only the best will play during the regular season. The coach looks for certain types of players, well-rounded and solid in all phases of the game: forwards who shoot and rebound; guards who can quarterback the team and shoot; a center who rebounds, scores, and sets strong picks. Good defense is essential at any position.

A typical day at training camp includes two drill sessions and one team meeting. For the Boston Celtics, the first drill session runs from 10:00 A.M. to 12:00 noon. After a light lunch, players head back to the gymnasium for a second session that starts at 3:00 and ends at 5:00. The team meeting or skull session is held from 7:30 to about 9:00 P.M.

Training camp is tough. It's meant to be that way so that the coach can weed out players he feels can't help the team. Every year one or two young players show up thinking pro ball is "just another game," a different uniform, waving to the pretty ladies in the stands, and an instant scrapbook of bold headlines on the sports page. The coach makes it clear from the beginning that pro ball demands hard work and self-discipline.

About twenty-five men try out for a ball club that can keep only twelve. From this large group, management seeks replacements for retired veterans, for those players sold to another club, or, perhaps, for the individual who has not improved. Some hopefuls, whatever their desires, soon discover they have not the skills to meet professional standards. Others find out that pro ball requires too much work and decide they don't want to make a living that way. The remaining few that depart are cut by management.

A new player is fighting to take another man's job. It is difficult to make friends with your rivals in this highly competitive situation. A player may have to remove emotional obstacles in order to perform effectively. Off the court, however, comradeship often develops. Horsing around helps to ease the pressure. In the evening, the dormitory halls echo with teasing, kidding voices and laughter resulting from a practical joke; in general, players cut up like a group of youngsters. These pleasant interludes occupy a small portion of time, however, between immersions in the pressure cooker. When training camp ends, the competition continues — for playing time.

Taping eliminates turning, so everyone must have his ankles taped to cut down on injuries. With twenty-five men at training camp and two daily practice sessions, there are 100 ankles per day for a trainer to tape.

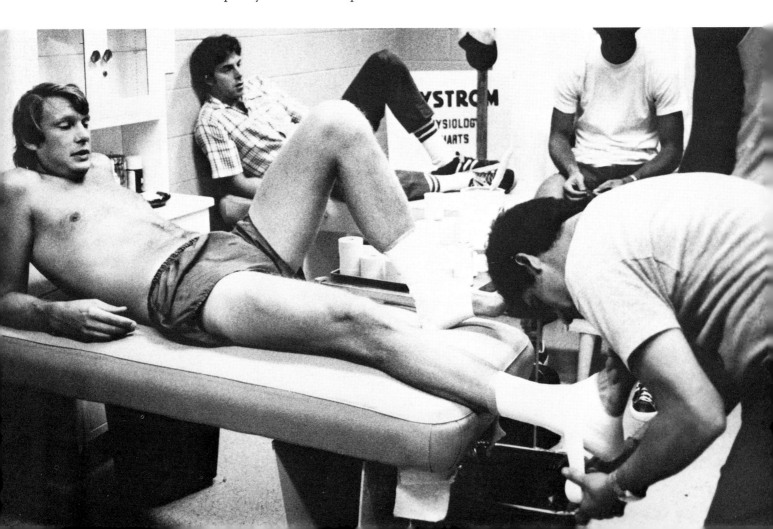

The average weight loss for a player during a two-hour practice session is three to five pounds. During a regular-season game a man can lose five to ten pounds. Most of it is lost through perspiration and should be gained back within twenty-four hours by drinking liquids and taking salt pills.

Feet are a *long way* down on the first day of training camp.

Randy (the assistant manager) has given me socks that are too small again!

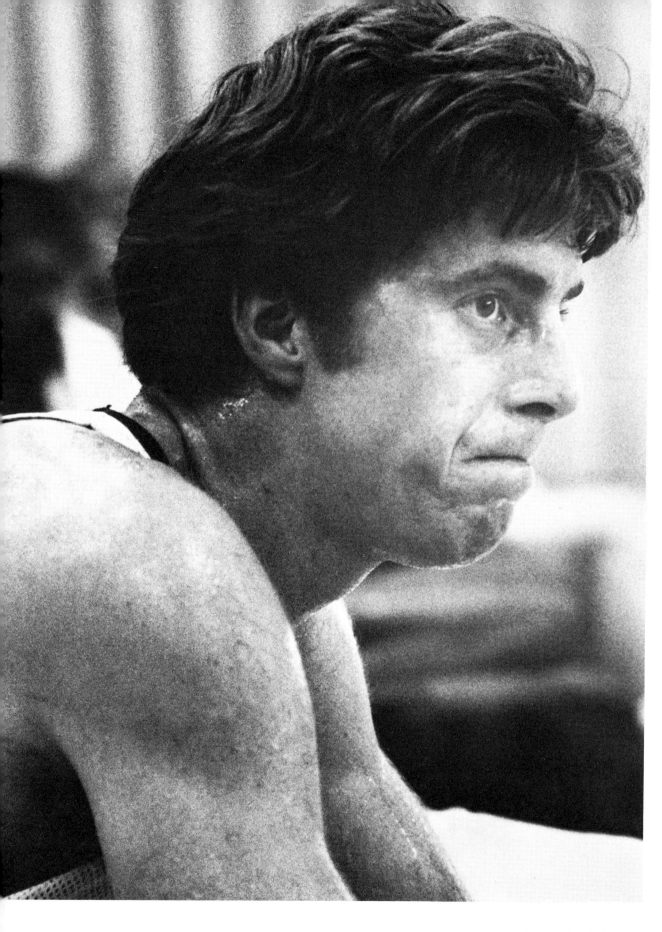

Hey, that wasn't a bad move.

The coach says, when you go to the hoop keep your arm out, protect the ball, and take a long stride.

Scrimmage is the last part of the drill session.

Eating is very important to put weight back on. Eat light close to practices, but fruits and juices give energy.

The first day of training camp — press day — is the easiest and most exciting for a rookie. He dons his fresh Celtic uniform for the first time. Newspaper reporters gather in clusters, scribbling his words into their notebooks. Radio announcers thrust microphones in front of him to catch what he says. Television cameras are pointed at him. Within this general chaos of media day, veterans gossip about the summer and complain about the fit of their uniforms. Rookies are more subdued; after all, most of them will depart long before the first snowfall.

On the second day, everyone sizes up the competition. Rookies see who they have to beat out; veterans speculate about new threats.

The third day, one veteran curses the long summer and wonders if the exercises he did on his own in August were enough. Leg muscles cry out under the strain. A rookie smiles; he's young and lithe.

The fourth day . . . Summer's lazy hours take their toll. Veterans' aches and pains multiply. They wonder if playing basketball is worth this agony. More sit-ups. More push-ups. More running, more running. Rookies now have their chance to outshine the veterans because they are already in good shape from playing in the summer leagues; but those damn drills are hard work and one or two newcomers in the rear of the exercise lines start to dog it under the illusion that no one notices.

By the fifth day, every twist of the body produces muscle aches and groans for both veteran and rookie. One veteran mutters about his "hustle scars." The swirling water of a whirlpool treatment and the relaxing embrace of a hot bath bring some relief.

On the sixth day, stiff reluctant muscles grow more limber. The body responds with less protest to mental commands.

It is the seventh day now. The veterans begin to show their stuff. They're ready to play ball. Practice becomes more intense.

On the eighth day, the coach starts to form various playing combinations, matching those athletes who work well together. The better ballplayers hang around together off the court and other men try to earn membership in that group.

By the ninth day, the rookie or veteran either belongs to the right combination or begins to feel threatened.

All this time, players' work has not ended with sunset. Each night, the coach conducts a skull session.

It's not that I'm goofing off, it's just that I did the exercises faster than anyone else.

A younger player is happy with his body at training camp. Older players have a tougher time of it.

When playing basketball, even in a scrimmage, play as hard and as well as you can.

WOW!

The Skull Session

There is more to professional basketball, as Tom Sanders says, than running, jumping, and shooting. Much planning goes into all maneuvers on the court. Evening skull sessions at training camp are classroom situations in which the coach and his assistant present different techniques of play.

With pencil and notebook in hand, players watch the coach chalk plays on the blackboard and explain when and why they are used against other teams. These plays are coordinated movements the team wants to make to shut off opponents, control the ball, and score.

The coach also shows game films from the previous year to better illustrate the desired moves on the court. In the flickering half darkness, players see offensive and defensive options that will click against whatever patterns or maneuvers the opposition throws at them. Rookies take it all in because this is their first detailed look at the team plays. If they learn them well, they can begin to anticipate action on the court.

Most of a player's actions must spring from spontaneous decisions. Repetition in practice and skull sessions imprints the set plays in an athlete's mind and allows him to perform instinctively on the court. If he pauses to think about every move, he is lost.

The veteran has become familiar with most of the plays in previous years. The repetition serves as a refresher course for him, although there will be an occasional new wrinkle. His chief role consists in asking sharp questions in the general discussion to help the rookie along.

The final test is on the court.

Films are used to show how plays are made.

The informal classroom session allows players to stretch out after the exhausting day-time practices and to keep minds alert for new plays.

One-two, one-two, ugh! One-two, one-two.

Shaping the Team

While the coach is working everyone into shape, the trainer is concerned with keeping everyone healthy. Players with a history of injuries (weak ankles, knee or back problems) have alerted him so that he can provide the proper safeguards (taped ankles, knee braces, exercises to strengthen the back). The routines of the trainer are intended to protect the players from aggravation of old injuries or the development of any new problems.

During the second week, the team begins to take shape. Some big cuts are made. Players learn they have been cut from the team when they keep an appointment with the management. Word of dismissal can come from the general manager as well as the coach. The management usually explains to a player why they think he cannot help the team as much as someone else. If they believe the player has potential and needs more experience, they may try to place him with a team in either the semipro or European leagues. The player cut from an NBA squad has open to him several avenues to a basketball career. If he is reluctant to find some other way to make a living, he can try the American Basketball Association, Eastern Professional League, Western League, Industrial League, or even the Harlem Globe Trotters, as well as the European Leagues.

The team now numbers fifteen players. They begin to learn each other's style and quirks. The athletes are grouped in certain units. Arrangements are made to take advantage of an individual's talent. For instance, a left-hander may set up, offensively, on the right-hand side of the court to give himself room to drive and to shoot on his strong side. The coach works his players at different positions to assess their versatility and to determine whether the team will be able to use many different offensive and defensive patterns or will be limited in style.

Everyone still with the club has a job to do and something to prove. A rookie must work his hardest to stay in the competition. The average player, age twenty-five to twenty-nine, has to perform well enough to keep himself from being used as trade bait. If a man has reached his early thirties, with the crest of his career behind him, he must play hard and stay in top-flight condition, since he knows his days are numbered. If the athlete has achieved star ranking, like Dave Cowens or Jo Jo White of the Celtics, and has done it all, he still has something to prove. Management expects consistently great things from him. And if he wants to hold the respect of his teammates, he'll have to show them why he has that multi-year contract, high salary, and all-star reputation.

With the start of exhibition games in the third week of training camp, players feel a sense of relief. They have escaped the initial cuts. The routine of camp changes to travel on the road and competition against other teams. More importantly, especially for the rookie, the probability of sticking in pro ball increases: other teams see him perform in these games and may offer him a chance to make their squads if he is dropped by the club he's trying out with. During the course of eight exhibition games, management cuts three more players, paring the team to the required 12-man regular-season roster.

As the schedule of exhibition games draws to a close, the team develops its working units, dependent upon strengths of its own players and styles of the opposition. The athletes grow tired of playing games that don't count in the final standings and of scrimmaging against each other. Tempers flare quickly as the opening of the regular season approaches. Finally game uniforms are distributed. Training camp has ended.

A rookie thinks to himself, "My time is coming. I'll show these veterans how to play."

Missing a medical or a dental appointment can be detrimental to a player's health. A fine is issued for missing an appointment.

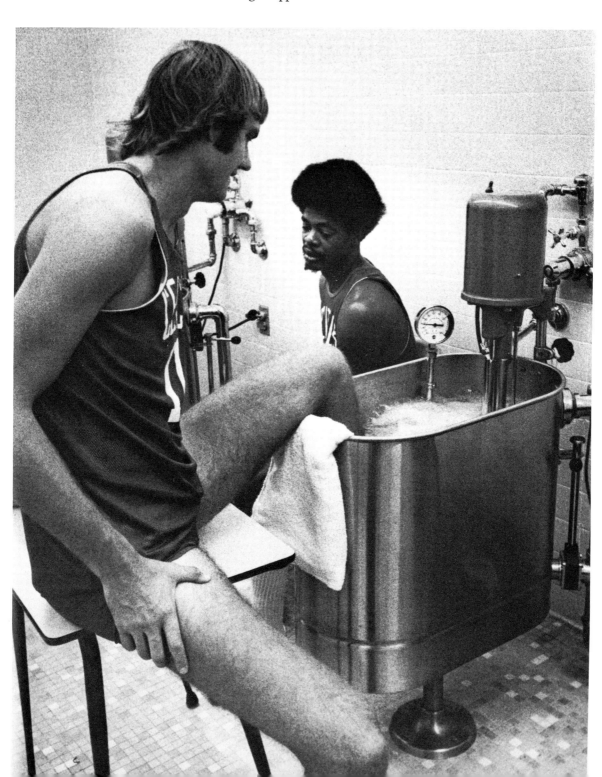

Fines

A list of rules and regulations is given to the players at the beginning of the year by the coach and if not followed will result in a player's being fined. These fines are imposed to instill discipline and good performance.

All money collected in this way is taken out of the players' expense money and put into a common kitty which is used for a party at the end of the year.

Rules vary with the different clubs. The following are Celtic rules:

Curfew for training camp is at 12:00 midnight. During the regular season, players are expected to be in their rooms within two and one-half hours after the games. If this rule is not kept, a fine will be levied, the amount to be at the coach's discretion.

Missing practice, $100.

Coming late to practice, $1 per minute.

Missing a public appearance or a speaking date, $100.

Missing medical, dental, or trainers' appointments, $100.

Missing air flights, the cost of air fare plus $100.

A Celtic is expected to look like a champion. Suit jackets are worn on all trips and to and from all arenas. Fine for non-adherance is $100.

No socks will be issued until a pair has been turned in.

For non-return of uniform and warm-up gear at the first team meeting following each road trip, $25.

Lateness for bus, $1 per minute.

Charges for lost uniforms, pants — $25; shirt — $30; warm-up jackets — $45; warm-up pants — $35.

No friends are allowed in the locker room unless cleared in advance.

Suitcases are provided for travel. They must be used.

A word to the wise about injuries: report them promptly to the trainer. The sooner he gets at it, the sooner the player will be back in action. This is very important at training camp. The coach can only go by the performance he sees.

Personal expenses incurred at hotels while traveling must be paid by the individual player when he checks out, otherwise charges will be deducted in double from salary checks.

Beer in moderation, hard liquor and wines out. Fine is $50 per drink.

The start of the season begins with the distribution of game uniforms.

What size do you wear? Do you like them close or loose, heavy or light, high cuts or low cuts?

Before the Game

Players arrive in the locker room about two hours before game time. In the next hour and a half, they change from street clothes to their uniforms, visit the trainer to have their ankles taped and receive whatever special care they may need, and wait. Some athletes nap, while others may walk out to the court early, before any spectators have entered the building, to take some extra shooting practice.

About thirty-five minutes before the start of the game, the coach must make sure his team is in the proper mood to perform at peak efficiency. The first game of the season is the easiest for which to prepare a team mentally because every athlete is anxious to play. Most players have pride and give everything they have when they are in the game. This professional spirit makes it unnecessary for a coach to "psych up" a team for all eighty-two games. His effort may be necessary only eight to ten times a season. For instance, when the Celtics return from a long road trip to play at home against a supposedly weak team, coach Tom Heinsohn may discuss pride and the importance of *every* game in order to insure against a letdown and a flat performance.

Before every game, the coach calls for attention. Players gather at their dressing areas, some standing, some reclining, others sitting on chairs. Discussion begins. The plays of tonight's opposition (many of which are familiar to the veterans from previous seasons, all of which have been scouted by the assistant coach) take shape on the blackboard. The athletes discuss the other team position-by-position; they analyze their own strengths and weaknesses as well as those of the opposition.

Each player also considers his individual assignment. Since the zone defense is outlawed in the NBA, all teams must play man-to-man. This rule means that each game consists of a series of match-ups. A center who tonight confronts a strong defensive center on the other team may remind himself to fake the shot before releasing the ball when driving to the hoop in order to draw the defender out of position or to force him to commit a foul. If his opponent plays an extremely physical game, the center thinks he may have to fire out an elbow or two early in the night to let the other guy know he's not going to wilt under the leaning and pushing.

Perhaps the other club starts a rookie at one of the forward positions. The forward matched against the rookie wants to test him, find out what the newcomer can do. This forward, then, will look for his shot more quickly tonight; attempt to establish his superiority at once; and intimidate the rookie with some strong physical play or his sharpest move.

And let's say, as is frequently the case, one of the opposition's guards is nursing a bad leg. He has suffered a minor injury, but the trainer has taped his leg and he will try to play. The guard paired against this man believes he can take advantage of the injury. He plans to "punish" the injured guard, make him run all the time and work harder on defense, tire him out quickly and force the opposing coach to replace him with a less skilled substitute. This strategy may sound cruel, but it merely reflects the intensity of play and the importance of every condition in determining the winner of the game. The other team, in a locker room down the hall, mulls over the same thoughts about the players on *this* team.

Meanwhile a rookie who normally receives little playing time hopes his team will blow the opposition right off the court so that he'll get an opportunity to perform. An older veteran wants to get into the action early; if he sits too long on the bench, his muscles may stiffen up and he won't play at his best when the coach inserts him in the line-up until he has warmed up again by running down the court a few times. This problem is common to many players and explains the great value placed by a coach on a good "sixth man" — a reserve who responds immediately when placed in the game.

Pregame talk draws to a finish. Teammates clasp hands, seeming to gain strength from each other; some players pray. In these final moments of privacy, one player applies a strip of tape to a sore finger, another adjusts his knee brace, a third chews a candy bar for added energy. As part of the delicate balance of mental preparation, many teams respect the superstition that lining up to go out to the court in a certain order each night can bring good luck. With the coach's parting words, "let's get off to a good start," ringing in their ears, the players file out of the locker room. More than one coach believes that, to a large extent, the upcoming game already has been won or lost, depending upon the mood created by these quiet locker room hours.

I may not have the ball but my man's not going anywhere.
Just eighty-one more games to go after tonight.

The closer to the basket you get the less room there is.

I've got to keep my man away from that ball.

Basketball, a noncontact sport?
I could pass the ball over my shoulder, but that would be a blind pass.

Offensive foul — it looked like Havlicek stepped into me.

I should have blocked him out farther from the basket. Now he has as much of a chance at the board as I do.

His stance is too wide and he's up too high.
I think I'll go to my right.

1820785

The Game

Down the runway and out on the floor the players trot. Wearing their warm-up suits, they run through lay-up drills and spread out on the court, each working on the shots he will take during the game.

From the moment the team steps on the floor, the crowd reacts. As the pre-game warm-ups continue, spectators file in to fill the thousands of seats in the auditorium. In the outer lobby, a last-minute scalper offers "two at courtside."

Each player handles his nervousness, worry, and mental preparation in a different way. To some the crowd noise is faraway, to others it is an integral part of the mounting tension.

The buzzer sounds a long note accompanied by a rising cheer of expectation from the crowd. High above the court, rows of television lights are shining brightly. The starters pull off their warm-up togs, listening all the while to the coach's final instructions. The public address announcer calls out each player's name and cheers or boos from the crowd resound throughout the building. Players fidget with eagerness as the organist thunderously plays the national anthem.

Tonight, the Celtics face the New York Knickerbockers before a capacity crowd at Boston Garden. Dave Cowens bends through last-minute exercises and joins his teammates at center court. The referee tosses the ball high in the air and the game is on.

The players rip into action. Knicks Bill Bradley and Phil Jackson muscle their way through the forecourt. Don Chaney slams past a pick to hound Walt Frazier. A shot bounces high off the rim and a forest of straining arms, above a grunting collision of bodies, fights for the rebound. Cowens clutches the ball and flings the outlet pass to John Havlicek, who races toward the other end, one hand dribbling the ball, the other waving his teammates upcourt. Tom Heinsohn is up off the bench, urging, "Run, run!"

A white wave, a controlled charge, the Celtics sweep downcourt, filling the fast break lanes. A fake, a perfect pass to the flying Jo Jo White, who gathers in the ball and lays it up softly against the glass in one smooth balletic motion.

"Basket by White from Havlicek," the public address announcer calls out.

Long hot hours on the court and concentrated mental effort in the skull sessions made that play possible. Each Celtic fulfilled a predetermined role. The x's and o's scribbled in chalk on a blackboard back in September have become running, jumping flesh-and-blood here in the regular season.

Players react almost instinctively during a game. There is no time to hesitate, pondering "What now?" Part of any team's strategy involves making the opposition think, foiling their habitual patterns, forcing them to react in ways that maximize its own advantage.

The game rolls on, the edge swinging back and forth. Along the sidelines, reporters watch the action and peck at typewriters. Cameras click and whir. A rebound battle ends with 500 pounds of basketball players prone on the floor. As the two centers slowly regain their feet, a ballboy races out with a towel to wipe up the wet spot on the court. Popcorn vendors and radio announcers are shouting. With a high-arcing, full-court heave of the ball as the buzzer sounds, the half ends.

The fifteen-minute half time is the only sustained break players receive in a game. Teams rest, regroup, consider the flow of the game to this point, and make whatever adjustments are necessary. Then, it is back out to the floor.

Havlicek calls the play, loud and clear, hand over head: "Thirty-three." The Celtics cut, set picks, swerve toward the basket hoping to get open for a back-door pass. The Knicks shut off the lanes, jump out on switches at the picks, keep their hands up, apply pressure to force a turnover. All the while both teams are grunting, pushing, talking to teammates, yelling at the referees. "He's holding me, Manny!"

The two officials play a major role in this continuous foot race, wrestling match, and chess game. They attempt to stay in good position to see everything that is happening and to make the proper calls of fouls and violations. They are running with the teams all night and flying around the country all season on schedules of their own no newspaper publishes and no fan knows.

The Celtics put on a burst late in the fourth quarter and grab a five-point lead with only three minutes left. The Knicks call a time out. A team can suddenly develop momentum — a short stretch of the game when it controls the pace, finds a high percentage of its shots dropping through the hoop, and, in general, confuses the other team's pattern of attack and defense. The time out is a key weapon a coach uses against a team riding high with momentum. It is hoped this sixty-second break will cool off the other team and allow his own club to regroup. Each team may call only seven time outs in a game, however (and no more than four in the last period), so they must be used carefully. The coach and players talk over what's working, what's not working, what adjustments must be made or what should be remembered.

Tonight, the Knicks' time out fails to slow down the Celtics. Don Chaney dribbles away the final seconds of the game out near midcourt. With the cheers of the home crowd escorting them, the players head to the locker room.

I've really set him up for my reverse dribble.

The final, frantic rush to get the final statistics out before the next quarter begins.

Blocked shot!

National Basketball Association
Official Scorers Report

Date Oct. 26, 1973   At   Boston Garden   Attendance 15,320 (capacity)
Officials Don Murphy - Jerry Loeber   Time   2:00 p.m.

Visitors New York Knicks	Min. Played	Goals Made	- Att.	Free Throws Made	- Att.	Rebounds Off	-Def	-Tot	Assists	Personals	Steals	Points
17 Bibby	14	5	7	2	2	2	1	3	2	2	1	12
24 Bradley	37	6	15	1	2	1	1	2	2	5	1	13
31 Davis	1	0	0	0	0	0	0	0	0	0		0
22 DeBusschere	Did not Play Injured Knee Did Not Dress ←											
10 Frazier	45	9	18	3	5	2	7	9	4	2	1	21
14 Garrett	9	0	0	0	0	0	0	0	0	0		0
40 Gianelli	DNP											
18 Jackson	35	7	13	2	2	0	3	3	4	5		16
32 Lucas	21	0	4	0	0	0	0	0	2	2		0
7 Meminger	32	6	12	2	2	1	3	4	2	1		14
19 Reed	30	7	11	4	4	2	5	7	3	3		18
43 Wingo	16	3	7	1	2	2	2	4	1	3		7
Totals	240	43	87	15	19	10	22	32	20	23	3	101

FG% 49%   FT% 78%   Turnovers 18 - 18 pts Team Rebounds: 6

Home Boston Celtics	Min. Played	Goals Made	- Att.	Free Throws Made	- Att.	Rebounds Off	-Def	-Tot	Assists	Personals	Steals	Points
12 Chaney	38	5	8	0	0	0	0	0	4	5	1	10
18 Cowens	45	12	18	5	6	2	15	17	5	5		29
32 Downing	DNP											
19 Finkel	DNP											
20 Hankinson	DNP											
17 Havlicek	45	15	23	4	8	2	2	4	9	3		34
11 Kuberski	16	6	7	3	3	0	1	1	0	2		15
19 Nelson	16	1	4	2	2	1	1	2	0	2		4
15 Silas	29	3	8	2	2	5	9	14	4	4		8
44 Westphal	6	0	1	1	2	0	0	0	0	2	2	1
10 White	45	5	12	2	2	2	2	4	6	3		12
7 Williams	DNP											
Totals	240	47	81	19	25	12	30	42	28	26	3	113

FG% 58%   FT% 76%   Turnovers 22 - 21 pts. Team Rebounds: 8

Blocked Shots					Scored Points	1	2	3	4	OT	OT	OT	Total
Visitors: N.Y.		Home:Boston			Boston	27	21	29	36				113
Bradley	2	Nelson	1		New York	26	25	21	29				101
		White	1		Remarks: Tech Jackson 04:11; Tom Heinsohn								
		Silas	1		8.44 3rd period								
	2		3										

42

"But, Gentlemen, I don't think you saw the play."

During a time out perspiration is mopped up, off the playing floor.

This play will never be completed.

Players listen to the coach recount their mistakes.

Enter the reporters. (Photos by David Cowens)

After the Game

"That's the way to go, men!"

After the game, players and coach discuss mistakes that made the victory more difficult. Reporters surge in. They stop first to talk with the coach; then, unless someone else played exceptionally well, they visit captain John Havlicek. Don Nelson and Paul Silas get their turns. Jo Jo White, sitting beside Havlicek at his locker, shares the comments. Dave Cowens retires to the trainer's room to rest. Quick questions pass through the crowd of reporters and players after a big game. A player leans back against his locker. In front of him, the knot of writers hovers, scrawling his words into notebooks.

"What about Frazier?"

"Well, he's so great you can't hope to stop him every night. Sometimes you get lucky..."

"Did they surprise you with that defensive shift in the third quarter?"

"No. We adjusted right away..."

The questions flow out: about high scorers, low scorers, air balls, stuffs, and steals; about planned plays and why did you slip?

Eventually, some reporters hurry away to file their stories before deadline. Players, their words already on the way into print and destined to be read by thousands with tomorrow morning's coffee, head for the showers. A photographer snaps a headshot to place in his files or to accompany a special story. In a separate room, television cameras turn on their bright lights and record interviews for the late news. (No tape recorders are permitted in the locker room so that private comments cannot be lifted out of context.)

The athletes begin to unwind and rap with each other about the game. Hank Finkel looks up, observant; Jo Jo White laughs; Art Williams throws in a wisecrack or two; Don Nelson chuckles. John Havlicek says something to Don Chaney, who shakes his head and laughs. The rookies often don't take part because they've not played. The trainer hands out tape cutters and salt pills, works on cramps, checks old and new injuries.

The players get dressed and, singly and by twos, emerge from the locker room to greet waiting wives and friends. Perhaps one or two youngsters, the last remainder of the night's huge crowd of spectators, linger outside the door in hope of autographs. Players find their cars in the near deserted parking lot. Boston Garden is dark and silent.

On the road again.

ITINERARY

The Longest Road Trip...

Boston Celtics West Coast Travel Itinerary---

Thurs.   3:50 p.m. depart Boston--dinner on plane
          arriving in Houston at 7:40 p.m.
          Bus to hotel

Fri.   8:00 p.m. vs Houston at the Hofheinz Pavilion

Sat.   6:30 a.m. bus from hotel to airport
          8:05 a.m. depart Houston--breakfast on plane
          arriving in Phoenix at 10:16 a.m.
          Cab to hotel
          8:00 p.m. vs. Phoenix at the Vets Memorial Coliseum

Sun.   10:45 a.m. depart Phoenix
          arriving in Los Angeles at 10:49 a.m.
          Cab to hotel
          7:00 p.m. vs Los Angeles at the Forum

Mon.   10:15 a.m. depart Los Angeles
          arriving in Oakland at 11:15 a.m.
          Hotel

Tues.   8:05 p.m. vs. Golden State at Oakland Coliseum Arena

Wed.   12:25 p.m. depart Oakland--snack on plane
          arrive Portland at 1:49 p.m.
          Hotel
          5:00 p.m. practice

Thurs.   1:00 Practice

Fri.   8:00 p.m. vs. Portland at Portland Memorial Coliseum

Sat.   9:00 a.m. bus from hotel to airport
          10:35 a.m. depart Portland
          arriving in Seattle at 11:08 a.m.
          Bus to hotel

Sun.   4:30 p.m. bus from hotel to Seattle Center Coliseum
          7:00 p.m. vs. Seattle at Seattle Center Coliseum
          Bus to hotel following the game

Mon.   7:00 a.m. bus from hotel to airport
          8:00 a.m. depart Seattle--breakfast on plane
          arriving in Boston at 5:50 p.m.

Traveling really gets to you.

How can you have three tens when I have two of them!

This is the way the weather should be all the time.

Road Trip

It's a cold wind that whips off the Charles River in Boston's winter. In fact, most of the Celtics' road trips in the East and Midwest lead to frozen cities. When the long-awaited extended journey to the West Coast finally turns up on the schedule, most players welcome it with enthusiasm.

Professionally, the West Coast trip is a difficult challenge. The Pacific Division is loaded with good teams like the Los Angeles Lakers, Golden State Warriors, and Seattle Supersonics; all of them can be tougher to beat on their home courts. Nonetheless, the prospect of warmer weather for a week or two bestows a glow of pleasure on the trip. Players nurse the wild hope that upon their return home, just maybe the Northeast winter will have ended early. No chance.

The player searches through his wardrobe and picks out his summer clothes. A full suitcase is light this time around.

The long flight across the continent is more relaxing now in newer and larger planes like the 747. In first class, the basketball player finds enough room to walk around standing straight. He can sit comfortably in his seat without fear that the person in front of him will tilt back the seat and jam his knees up around his chest. Players fill the idle hours of flight playing cards, reading, or sleeping.

Most hotels, however, are not prepared to cater to men taller than a few inches over six feet. Result: small beds, small bathtubs, and shower heads that spray water no higher than a player's navel. The player may find it difficult to relax in peace. Many hotels allow telephone calls from fans to ring through to the players, thus disturbing them in the middle of sleep or private preparation for the evening's game. Youngsters come knocking at the athletes' doors at strange hours or congregate in groups around the lobby in search of autographs.

Because the food served in most hotel dining rooms is expensive and not available late at night when the players return from the game, most players seek out various restaurants in town. Expense money (to cover the costs of dining and entertainment) is currently nineteen dollars per day.

In their free hours, some players lie around the pool (no swimming, however, because water induces too great a relaxation of the muscles); others sleep, watch television, read, shop, take in a movie, or eat a light meal. Sleep helps to prepare the player for the game. On the road, with family and friends absent, he may get more rest than at home.

The three-hour time difference between Boston and the West Coast and the sudden change to lazy weather make the first game of this long trip the most difficult. In addition, the players must contend with the disadvantages of playing on another team's home court.

Jeers and boos of hostile fans can inspire visiting players because it's fun to beat the home team and silence the crowd. The crowd's cheers, however, can often spark the *home* team, especially in the heat of a closely contested fourth quarter. Foreign courts may conceal dead spots, undiscovered by the visiting players until one of them causes a turnover at a crucial moment. The floor may be slippery; it may be too hard and require an altered style of dribbling. Drafts swirl through some arenas. In other auditoriums, unfamiliar colors or lighting may affect a player's shooting.

After the game, local reporters often tend to see with home-oriented eyes. Even though the visiting team played and won a good game, the writers sometimes search for consolations for their team. They may take comfort in the closeness of the score or attribute the winning hoop to luck, wizardry, or the whim of an unjust god.

Leaving the locker room, visiting players are greeted by fans thrusting forward autograph books, noisy grudge bearers heckling from the shadows, and perhaps even hard flying objects. As far as many fans are concerned, *visitors* means enemy.

There is another problem involved with a long road trip. Most players are married; many have young children. Travel places added stress upon a family since the husband is away from the home more than 100 days a year. As a public figure, he has minimal privacy. Even when he returns home he may not be able to devote as much time as he would like to his family because he is physically exhausted from the grind of travel. Some wives do not mind the three- and four-day trips, as they have time to see friends. Wives usually dread the two-week trips, however, because of the father's extended absence from the children. Adjustments that must be made in family life when a man travels frequently are another part of a pro ball player's life.

No matter how much I try, I can't take my mind off this game.

I hope we get this back tap. At least here I can't lose the ball in the lights.

If he holds the ball in that position for another split second I'll be right on it.

Lord deliver me from these bad officials.

When you put this type of pressure on the pass, it's bound to be off target.

It sure helps to have strong shoulders and arms.

When giants collide something's got to give.

Don't leave the ball behind your head when rebounding — it's vulnerable.

When dribbling, a player should keep his head up and protect the ball with his free hand.

Defense should be played with the feet, but I think I'll use my arm a little.

Tight nets can really slow up a fast break.

Whew! A sigh of relief! Close games can really exhaust a fan.

Home Again

The bright-white Celtic home uniform dazzles the eyes after so many games wearing dark green. The fans are excited to see their team back home. For the player, it feels good to perform once again in front of people who are on his side. Although Boston Garden is home, there exists minimal advantage for the Celtics since they practice at Lexington Academy. Fans and one's friends make the court feel like home.

The team approaches and soon passes the midpoint of the season. Over the course of forty or fifty games, the players, individually and as a unit, experience many peaks and valleys in their game. The individual player suffers most when he falls into a slump — a time during which he plays poorly throughout several consecutive games. A slump turns tighter the screws of pressure on a player because the team defines its style based, in part, on his skill; also, his contract for next season depends on his consistent performance. A player who suddenly finds he can't score may attempt to help his club by bearing down harder on defense and passing more until his shooting touch returns.

To lighten his heavy thoughts, there is much fooling around in the locker room. His teammates tease an athlete if he dove for the ball and, instead, grabbed an ankle. He's mocked in good humor if his timing was off and he leaped for the rebound when the ball wasn't there. If he was faked out of position or missed three or four shots in a row, he may be entertained with imitations of his actions.

Nothing, however, not even a slump, lasts forever. Eventually, a man starts to play at his peak again. He fears disrupting a hot streak, for he knows only too well how easily it can be doused. Therefore, an athlete wants to behave in the same way when he is playing well. He may exercise the same way, dress the same way, even hang his street clothes in his locker in the same manner. When, inevitably, something does go wrong, a player may say: "Damn, I knew I hung my pants the wrong way." Players lean on superstition and continuity of habit. And there is truth in this tendency. The athlete's body is a finely tuned instrument; any disturbance can throw off his performance.

This is the way to rebound, two hands on the ball and look to the side the rebound came from.

It's a cinch this won't be a soft landing.

And they say the little man doesn't belong in this game!

A time out is called to reorganize the strategy.

Playoff Time

An NBA team's style of play during the last ten or fifteen games of the regular season depends upon its position in the divisional standings.

Some clubs no longer have a chance to qualify for the playoffs; they begin to plan for the next season, evaluating the performance of aging veterans and perhaps giving their rookies and younger players more time on the court.

If a team finds itself in a frantic race for a play-off spot, however, these late-season games carry the importance of the play-offs themselves. Regulars may play forty-eight minutes at high intensity to insure key victories.

A few teams already have locked up play-off berths. They can no longer be overtaken. In this case, coach and players want to use the final games of the season to prepare for the play-offs. While the coach may take the opportunity to rest some of his important veterans more frequently, experiment with various new combinations, and provide his bench with more playing time, the winning of games is still important. Home-court advantage in the play-offs goes, in each series, to the team with the better record. Playing the seventh game of the championship series at home may give a team the slight edge it needs to win the title. Also, no team wants to tumble into sloppy habits and a losing streak right before the play-offs.

The "Second Season," as the play-offs are sometimes called, begins with quarter-final round games about three days after the regular season ends. Eight teams qualify. The four winners of quarter-final series advance to the conference finals. The two survivors clash in the championship round. All series are best-of-seven matches. Thus, the eventual NBA champion wins twelve games in the Second Season.

Many people, including the players, feel that regular season accomplishments mean nothing if a team stumbles in the play-offs. For instance, the Celtics established a team record in the 1972-1973 season, winning sixty-eight of eighty-two games; however they lost the seventh game of the Eastern Conference play-offs to the New York Knicks, who went on to defeat the Lakers for the NBA championship. Few people mentioned the regular season record.

FOUL! I realize a defensive player should try to stop his man from getting to the base line, but this is ridiculous.

Everyone wanted to know: "What happened in the play-offs?"

In addition to the chance to become a champion, the play-offs offer an added incentive: money. Players on the NBA champion team each win approximately $20,000. This extra money (called the play-off pool) has increased each year. Runners-up in the finals earn about $14,000 per man. The Celtics usually vote some part of their play-off winnings to the trainer and front-office personnel.

In a short series, any team can catch fire and upset a supposedly superior team. Each game takes on added importance. If a club wins the opener, it can expect a tougher opponent in game two. The first-game loser studies films of the game, makes adjustments, resolves to bear down harder. By the third or fourth game of the series, there are few surprises either team can spring. The outcome rests in concentration and execution.

These Second Season games burden the player with additional pressure. Each game — and in a close series, each play — can determine how the player will spend his summer. Will he be in great demand, as a member of the NBA champions, for speaking engagements and endorsements? Or will he need to discover some off-season employment and answer inquisitions about how his team lost the play-offs? In addition, play-off games receive increased attention from fans and media. Newspapers assign extra reporters and photographers to cover the games; frenzied fans buy up tickets quickly, usually insuring sellout crowds; many games are beamed across the nation on television. The play-offs serve as the showcase of professional basketball.

By the second or third week in May, another season of pro ball has ended. Champagne flows in the dressing room of the NBA champion. The Celtics hope another green-and-white championship banner will hang from the rafters of the Boston Garden.

Outside, the sun grows warmer and the grass greener with the coming of summer. Players scatter to their homes, already beginning to think ahead: How good a contract can I sign for next season? Will the club draft some top players out of the college ranks? If I rest, will this injury heal? Rest. My body craves a rest.

Training camp is still several months away. Already, however, the new season has begun.

Don't leave the floor; get your hands up on the defense.

Because of the pressure of the game, many guys get their sports mixed up,

To take the charge you have to be there first and not move.

sometimes

very mixed up.

Eight inches taller and I'd reject that hook shot.

If penetration is what you want, penetration is what you'll get.

This is the closest last-second shot you can get in the last game of the Play-offs.

Postscript

As a player grows older and better, he plays more. Then, slowly, the muscles tighten up more easily and it takes a longer time to warm up. He finds it harder to do some of the things he once accomplished with ease. While he drives his body of thirty-four (or more) years to yield additional playing mileage, management starts looking for replacements (via the college draft, free agents, trade offers). Up-and-coming younger players need game experience in order to fit into the team's patterns. Slowly, inevitably, the veteran's playing time shrinks until he finds it difficult to compete at a level he enjoys. He sees it is time to get ready to take that painful step away from the enjoyable life of the professional basketball player.

Tom Sanders wasn't anticipating retirement until after the 1972-1973 season when he analyzed the situation. He realized that the addition of highly regarded forward Paul Silas, similar in playing style to "Satch" and an excellent rebounder) had made him a luxury the Celtics, perhaps, could not afford. Then, the Celtics drafted a potentially capable front-court pair in Steve Downing and Phil Hankinson. Sanders' choice became more clear. No doubt about it, a disease called retirement had set in.

Many years of playing basketball can exact a terrible toll from an athlete's body. His bone joints are worn, his ligaments stretched. Many infirmities supposedly reserved for old age (such as arthritis and rheumatism) set upon the player in his twenties. As his playing career nears its conclusion, the pro player discovers that some of his best friends are the trainers and doctors he sees with increasing regularity.

After leaving the game, the ex-athlete may lead a normal life but probably not an extremely physical one. He may have to pick his leisure sports with care.

If a professional athlete makes an effort to keep reasonably fit after his playing days are over, he can minimize dangers to his health and physical comfort and look forward to many productive years. He cannot, however, simply collapse into a rocking chair. His heart has become well-muscled during his basketball career. If he stops playing and also ceases to perform *any* physically demanding work or play, then he may, because of this prolonged inactivity, allow his well-muscled heart to grow fatty. Some doctors think a radical curtailment of exercise contributes to health problems later in an athlete's life.

The newly retired ballplayer is not cast adrift in the world when he leaves the game. The NBA Players' Association offers help, mainly in the form of severance pay, to an individual in settling into "civilian life." Upon retirement, a man receives approximately $3000 per year of play for a period of three years. For example if he played ten years, his severance pay is $30,000, sent to him within three years after he has left the game. This money helps the player move from the usually high-salaried status of a professional athlete to new beginnings in other money-making areas. In addition, a player may start to receive his pension (a sum of money based on the number of years he played in the league) in his middle fifties.

The professional basketball player does not disappear from productive life when he retires. Simply, he transfers his way of making a living to another field — he makes a career change. The ease of transition depends, primarily, on two factors. If, during college, he worked on academics as well as athletics and earned his diploma, and if he spent the off seasons during his pro career in some kind of useful employment, then now the ex-athlete is ready to make a contribution to society in another way.

The difficult, yet glory-filled, existence of the pro player has come to an end. It's just a matter of changing gears, however, and making what we like to call progress.

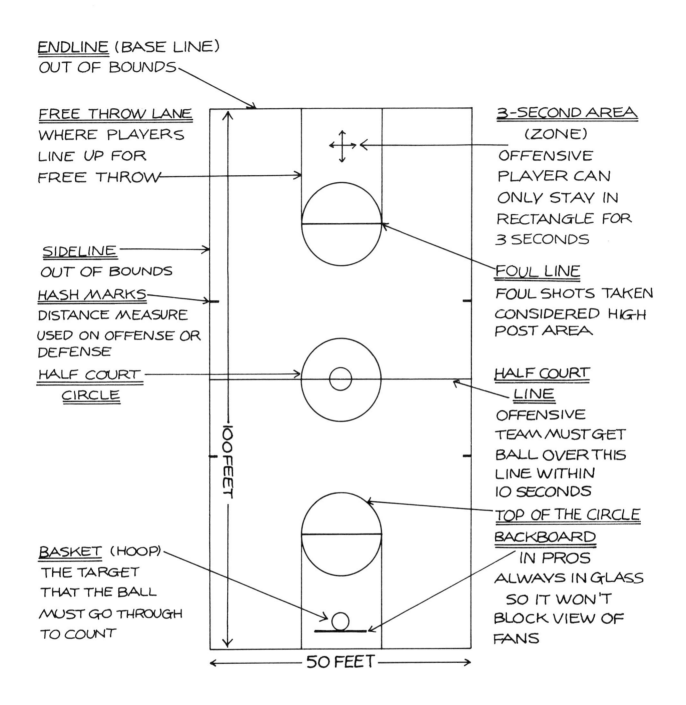

ENDLINE (BASE LINE)
OUT OF BOUNDS

FREE THROW LANE
WHERE PLAYERS
LINE UP FOR
FREE THROW

SIDELINE
OUT OF BOUNDS

HASH MARKS
DISTANCE MEASURE
USED ON OFFENSE OR
DEFENSE

HALF COURT
CIRCLE

100 FEET

BASKET (HOOP)
THE TARGET
THAT THE BALL
MUST GO THROUGH
TO COUNT

50 FEET

3-SECOND AREA
(ZONE)
OFFENSIVE
PLAYER CAN
ONLY STAY IN
RECTANGLE FOR
3 SECONDS

FOUL LINE
FOUL SHOTS TAKEN
CONSIDERED HIGH
POST AREA

HALF COURT
LINE
OFFENSIVE
TEAM MUST GET
BALL OVER THIS
LINE WITHIN
10 SECONDS

TOP OF THE CIRCLE
BACKBOARD
IN PROS
ALWAYS IN GLASS
SO IT WON'T
BLOCK VIEW OF
FANS

NORMALLY BACK COURT PLAYERS (GUARDS) PLAY IN AREA FROM FOUL
LINE TO HALF COURT LINE. FRONT COURT PLAYERS (FORWARDS)
PLAY IN AREA FROM TOP OF CIRCLE TO BASE LINE. PIVOT MEN
OR PLAYERS (CENTERS) PLAY AREA CLOSE TO BASKET - FROM
HIGH POST TO LOW POST IN 3-SECOND AREA (ZONE).

Glossary

BENCH: Those players sitting on the sidelines waiting to play. Also known as "reserves."

DEFENDERS: Players when on defense. They attempt to stop the team with the ball from scoring.

OFFENSIVE MEN: Players on the team with the ball who try to score by shooting the ball into the basket.

CENTER: Usually the tallest player on the team, he is expected to do much rebounding and scoring. He plays close to the basket, in and around the three-second zone.

GUARDS: Players normally concerned with running the team, passing, calling plays, and scoring. Frequently the shortest men on the team, they most often play the back-court positions from the foul line (extended) to the half-court line.

FORWARDS: Players normally in the front-court positions from the foul line (extended) to the base line, they rebound, score, and set picks.

COACH: Individual responsible for giving directions to the team. He also teaches players about the game.

TRAINING CAMP: Preseason activity during which players are worked into shape and evaluated by coach.

ROOKIE: Player with no previous pro experience. Usually a recent college graduate.

VETERAN: Player with at least one season of experience in pro basketball.

FREE AGENT: Player with no contractual ties to any pro basketball organization.

EXHIBITION GAME: Contest between two teams played before the start of the regular season in order, primarily, to test rookies and get players in shape.

SCRIMMAGE: Game played that does not count in league standings. Usually refers to intersquad game when players on the same team divide up and play against each other for practice.

TWENTY-FOUR-SECOND CLOCK: Device (usually two clocks, one located just beyond each base line to indicate how much time remains before the offensive team must shoot the ball at the basket. NBA team has twenty-four seconds in which to prepare its shot from the moment it gains possession of the ball. Penalty for failure to shoot is loss of possession. Clock starts over with each shot that touches basket area.

BOARDS: The backboard that supports each basket. Also known as "the glass" because backboards in pro ball are constructed of glass.

HOOP: Another term for basket or goal.

THREE-SECOND ZONE: Areas of court in vicinity of each basket, enclosed by foul line and free throw lanes, in which no offensive player may stay for more than three consecutive seconds. Penalty for violation: loss of possession of ball. Also known as "the lane."

REBOUND: Retrieval of ball by a player after a missed shot. Offensive rebound refers to capturing of the ball after a teammate's miss; defensive rebound, an opponent's miss.

AIR BALL: Colorful term to describe a shot that misses the rim, board, net — in fact, everything but the floor or someone's hands.

STUFF, DUNK, SLAM, OR JAM: Shot made by player by thrusting the ball downward through the iron rim of the basket into the net. Exceptionally high-percentage shot.

FAST BREAK: Offensive maneuver in which team gains possession of ball (frequently through missed shot by opposition) and attempts to get down court ahead of the defenders in order to score a lay-up or to set up an easy shot before the opposition can establish its defense. Also called "running game." Popular and effective style of play in pro basketball.

SWITCH: Two defenders exchanging defensive assignments to compensate for movements of offensive team (*see* Pick).

TURNOVER: Situation when offensive team loses possession of ball without taking a shot at basket.

STEAL: Situation when defensive player takes ball away from offensive man, frequently by surprise.

SET PLAY: Coordinated moves by a team on offense that have been prepared in advance and are intended to provide high-percentage shooting.

OUTLET PASS: Refers to action by player (who usually has just grabbed a defensive rebound) in throwing the ball to a teammate further upcourt. The quickness and accuracy with which this play is accomplished are considered essential to successful fast break offense (*see* Fast break).

CUT: Term referring to dismissal of member(s) of team by management. "Cut" also can mean an abrupt movement by offensive player, usually in direction of the basket, in an attempt to free himself from his defender.

ZONE DEFENSE: Pattern of defense in which players protect a specified area of court, guarding any offensive man who enters that area. Outlawed in the NBA.

MAN-TO-MAN DEFENSE: Pattern of defense in which each player guards a particular man on the offensive team wherever he goes (*see* Switch).

PICK (PICK AND ROLL): Pick refers to offensive player who positions himself as a barrier to prevent a teammate's defender from pursuing him. A basic component of any team's offensive pattern, the pick is designed to free an offensive player from his defender for an open shot. "Pick and roll" refers to situation in which the defender guarding the pick man switches to guard the freed offensive player and the pick man turns toward the basket in hope of receiving a pass and scoring a basket before another defender switches to guard him (*see* Switch).

PEP TALK: Short speech by coach, usually in locker room before a game, in which he attempts to prepare the players properly for the game. (Delivery of such a talk is called "psyching up" a team.)

SALT PILLS: Tablets ingested by player who has perspired a great deal. They replace the salt that leaves the body with the water of perspiration. Replacement of salt helps to prevent muscle cramps in the athlete.

BACK-DOOR PLAY OR PASS: Situation when offensive player, through certain moves (or "fakes"), draws his defender out of position and breaks for the basket hoping to receive a (back-door) pass and score before the defensive player can react.

GENERAL MANAGER: Individual responsible for administrative operation of the entire sports operation. One of his major duties is to handle contract negotiations with players.

NO-CUT CONTRACT: Agreement between team and player indicating that player cannot be dismissed for the contract period (frequently several years).

TRADE: Agreement between two teams to exchange two or more players.

DRAFT: Selection by pro teams, in reverse order of previous season's records (team with fewest victories picking first, champion of league choosing last), of college players who have completed their schooling. Intended to give weakest pro teams an opportunity to acquire best available new players.

FOUL: Two main categories: Personal fouls result from physical contact between players. Technical fouls are assessed to players (on the court or bench) or coach for unsportsmanlike conduct. Referees call all fouls. Personal fouls may result in free throws (unmolested shots taken from the foul line) for the player fouled. Technical fouls always result in one foul shot for opposition. Varieties of personal fouls include possession fouls (when defender initiates contact with offensive player not in the act of shooting), shooting fouls (defender initiates contact with offensive player in the act of shooting), offensive fouls (when offensive player, with or without the ball, initiates contact with defensive player), and loose-ball fouls (when player initiates contact with opponent when neither team controls the ball. Frequently called in rebound action). Double fouls occur when two players on opposite teams commit personal or technical fouls against each other at the same time.

LIST OF PLAYERS
As they appear in the photographs left to right